O DEATH, WHERE IS THY STING?

O Death,
WHERE IS THY STING?

Alexander Schmemann

TRANSLATED BY ALEXIS VINOGRADOV

ST VLADIMIR'S SEMINARY PRESS
CRESTWOOD · NEW YORK · 2003

LIBRARY OF CONGRESS CATALOGING-IN-PUBLICATION DATA

Schmemann, Alexander, 1921-1983.
  [Smert'! gde tvoe zhalo?. English]
  O Death, where is thy sting? / Alexander Schmemann ;
    translated by Alexis Vinogradov.
    p. cm.
  ISBN 0-88141-238-4
  1. Death—Religious aspects—Orthodox Eastern Church.
  2. Orthodox Eastern Church—Doctrines. I. Title.

BX323.S2413 2003
230′.19—dc21

2002037035

Copyright © 2003
St Vladimir's Seminary Press
575 Scarsdale Road · Crestwood · NY · 10707
1-800-204-2665

ISBN 0-88141-238-4

All Rights Reserved

Book illustration,
design, and cover by Amber Schley Houx

PRINTED IN THE UNITED STATES OF AMERICA

Contents

	Introduction	7
1	The Question of Death	13
2	The Last Enemy	21
3	The Origin of Death	29
4	The Resurrection of the Body	37
5	The Week of the Cross	45
6	Pascha	53
7	The Week of Anti-Pascha (Thomas Sunday)	63
8	The Nature of Man	71
9	The Religion of Salvation	79
	Appendix: Trampling Down Death by Death	89

Introduction

Near the snow, near the sun, in the highest fields,
See how these names are fêted by the waving grass
And by the streamers of white cloud
And whispers of wind in the listening sky.
The names of those who in their lives fought for
  life,
Who wore at their hearts the fire's center.
Born of the sun, they travelled a short while
  toward the sun
And left the vivid air signed with their honour.

—Stephen Spender, "I Think Continually
of Those Who Were Truly Great" (1936)

O DEATH, WHERE IS THY STING?

In their lexical currency the church fathers have left us this rare banknote: "A theologian is one who prays, and one who prays is truly a theologian." We can't redeem this treasure by a simpler explanation; it is itself an irreducible truth. If theology then is bordered within the mystery of prayer, a great theologian is perhaps the one who risks leaving the joy of his prayerful encounter to tell us what he has seen and heard. Among those who, in Spender's words above, "fought for life," Fr Alexander Schmemann is that rare, great theologian whose theology is always and only about life, for it is rooted in the One who is Life.

Not surprisingly, then, in a book about death, in these transcribed conversations delivered by Fr Alexander as broadcasts to Russia on Radio Liberty, there is so much more about life than death. There is no sentimental philosophizing here about death as illusion, or as some sad but necessary passage to another elusive but colorful

Introduction

afterlife. He sets squarely before us the apostle's affirmation, "The last great *enemy* is death!" and reminds us that at the tomb of his friend Lazarus, Jesus did not give a comforting sermon on how everything will be fine; rather, he reminds us of the evangelist's report that "Jesus wept." In these tears running down the cheeks of God lies the great lament over what the world has become and particularly what man has tragically accepted about himself and his own destiny, within a world that Fr Alexander unabashedly calls a "cosmic cemetery."

In this collection of talks we are not led comfortably and systematically down a corridor of neat proofs that will provide the definitive and last word on the subject of death. It is precisely the philosophical legacy of such systematic proofs, as Fr Alexander demonstrates, that they have added nothing to the perennial ambiguity about death but have produced instead an irreconcilable polarization of two worldviews that either reject this world in favor of an elusive other world, or simply deny death in a mad materialist progress into an equally elusive Utopia. It is Fr Alexander's "trademark" and familiar approach that he leads us instead toward the Church's liturgical and specifically Paschal mystery, where the meaning and transformation of death into life is revealed in the encounter with the One who is himself the Life of life.

Precisely because the Paschal mystery, and therefore the teaching concerning life and death, is at the core of Christian theology and experience, Fr Schmemann's whole teaching directly or indirectly alludes to the theme of death. We find echoes of his references here to the materialists and Feuerbach already in the introductory chapter of his landmark study, *For the Life of the World*. The sixth chapter of that volume, "Trampling Down Death by Death," we have included as a fitting epilogue to the present collection, but we also urge the reader to enjoy it within the

Introduction

framework of the original study. There he himself writes, "The whole life of the Church is in a way the sacrament of our death, because all of it is the proclamation of the Lord's death, the confession of his resurrection."[1]

In his broadcasts, Fr Alexander notes:

> In order to console himself, man created a dream of another world where there is no death, and for that dream he forfeited *this* world, gave it up decidedly to death.
>
> Therefore, the most important and most profound question of the Christian faith must be, How and from where did death arise, and why has it become stronger than life? Why has it become so powerful that the world itself has become a kind of cosmic cemetery, a place where a collection of people condemned to death live either in fear or terror, or in

O DEATH, WHERE IS THY STING?

> their efforts to forget about death find themselves rushing around one great, big burial plot?

These are the initial questions that launch us in this book toward the final Christian resolution of the age-old quandary and struggle with death.

* * *

The first four talks on death were consecutive in the order of broadcasts. The remaining talks in this book were given at different times and related to Pascha, the resurrection. They are included because they continue to disclose the theme of death in the light of the Christian teaching and liturgical experience of Pascha.

—Alexis Vinogradov

---

[1] Alexander Schmemann, *For the Life of the World* (Crestwood, NY: SVS Press, 1973) 104.

CHAPTER 1

The Question of Death

Today, let us boldly plunge into our subject directly, without detours. We must assert that in human consciousness the question about religion, about God, about faith, is directly related to the question of death. More precisely, it is related to the question of whether something

O DEATH, WHERE IS THY STING?

exists after death. This is the widespread and unrelenting question that continues to torment humanity about the meaning of this world and about life beyond the grave. Inasmuch as there is no scientific, that is to say, positive, self-evident, and provable evidence on this question, neither *pro* nor *contra*, the question remains perennial and open and continues to evoke a millennium's worth of passionate and boisterous controversy.

Indeed, those who actively oppose the existence of another world claim that they have scientifically proven the impossibility of a positive or scientific demonstration of the existence of anything whatsoever after death and the immortality of the soul. Of course all of these proofs can be debunked the way Vladimir Nabokov does in one of his tales (let us keep in mind that Nabokov himself is not a believer).

We find one of Nabokov's characters dying after a long and torturous illness, and in the few

The Question of Death

moments before death, as he regains lucidity after a prolonged torpor, the question comes back to torment him with full force: is there something there in the afterlife, or not? He lies in a room with closed shutters, and behind the window he can hear the gurgling of water. The dying man says to himself, "Of course there is nothing on the other side of life—I know this as surely as I know that rain is falling on the other side of this window." But in actual fact, continues Nabokov, the spring sun was shining, and as the tenant in the upstairs apartment was watering her plants, the water was dribbling down on the lower window. Nabokov cites the ironic list of all the so-called "proofs"—yes, obviously the rain is falling, yet clearly there is no rain, and actually the sun is shining.[1]

This is clearly why we do not turn to science for questions about life after death, about what happens after death. Obviously, this is not an area for science, for science concerns itself exclusively with this side of life, and all scientific methods, its instruments, its hypotheses, and its proofs and methodology, are directed and adapted to such concerns.

Where, then, can we look if not to science? To philosophy? It is true that from the beginning of time, at the outset of human thought, philosophy tried to furnish an ultimate answer to this tormenting question.

We have that famous dialogue of Plato, *Phaedo*, which is wholly dedicated to the proof of the immortality of the soul. It is probably one of the most profound books written on the subject. It is no accident that the hero of another literary work, in a novel of Aldanov, furtively looks for Plato's book before committing suicide: "Now I will finally learn if there's something there or not." In fact, he fails to find the book.[2]

It would seem that Plato's proof works for those who already believe in the immortality of the

The Question of Death

soul. In the whole history of mankind we certainly have not heard of any unbeliever in the immortality of the soul, having read Plato's *Phaedo*, suddenly exclaim, "Well, I didn't believe before, but having read Plato, I am certainly a believer now."

And we can probably say the same about all philosophical attempts at proving this question. The additional problem with all these proofs is that in their attempt to affirm the existence of another world, they in fact undermine the reality and the value of this visible world.

Plato says, "The whole life of a wise man is just one eternal dying." Plato's argument is that this world contains only suffering, only mindlessness, only change, which means that there must be another world, where there is happiness, where there is eternal life, where there is blessedness and changelessness. It is, of course, the perennial argument: things are awful here, therefore let us look forward to what awaits us on the other side.

Ironically, it is because of our cynicism and our rejection of the only world given to us, against this rejection, against its devaluing, against its demeaning, that a great revolt occurred in the world. It is precisely on account of such a view that man abandoned religion. For, can it really be that God created the world and life and all of its beauty, all of its possibilities, only in order that man would reject them and forego all these glorious possibilities in the name of some unknown and only vaguely promised *other* world? And the reasoning goes, "Well, since all religions are calling us to such an understanding—let's throw out religion altogether, we can survive well enough without it, we can live a far better life here on earth."

The result is that humanity seems to be divided into two camps, which are constantly in conflict

The Question of Death

with each other—and all on account of man's conception of death and its total ambiguity. Partisans of one camp, in defending that other world beyond the grave, truly belittle this world and its life; they yield to its meaninglessness and its evil, for they say that only in the other world one no longer finds meaninglessness or evil. The other camp defends this world; in the name of the now, it rejects any possibility of eternity, and in so doing it *de facto* reduces man to an accidental, transitory, and temporal occurrence.

But is it necessary to accept either of these positions as correct? Is it truly possible that the choice lying before us is really a choice between two meaningless affirmations? On one side it seems there is faith in a Creator-God—and at the same time, the rejection of his creation, the thirst to depart from this God-created world; and on the other side there is an affirmation of the world, yet a world that is horrible in its meaninglessness, for the one who alone has the

O DEATH, WHERE IS THY STING?

possibility of using and enjoying this world—man—is in this world an accidental guest, destined for total annihilation. And so this horrible and frightening dilemma brings us to the one question that each of us must pose: in the final analysis, how do *I* personally relate to this inescapable, universal, and relentless question about death?

Such are the issues that launch us into the discussion of the troubling and tormenting problem of death. Is it possible that the time has finally come for us to approach this issue with courage and with humility? Let us now turn to consider what answer to this question is given by the Christian faith, a faith built on the annihilation of death and on the resurrection.

[1]The character's name is Alexander Yakovlevich Chernyshevski. Vladimir Nabokov, *The Gift* (New York: Wideview/Perigree, 1963), p. 324.
[2]Mark Aleksandrovich Aldanov. *Samoubiistvo* [Suicide] (New York: Izd. Literaturnogo fonda, 1958).

CHAPTER 2

The Last Enemy

"The last enemy to be destroyed is death" (1 Cor 15:26)—these are the words of the apostle Paul, writing at the dawn of Christianity following the relentless persecution and death of Christ, in a time of a general, passionate hatred of Christians.

O DEATH, WHERE IS THY STING?

In my last conversation I said that the question about death and, more precisely, the *confusion about death,* lies at the very heart of human understanding, and in the final analysis, the relation of man to life, that which we call his worldview, is ultimately determined by his relationship to death. I also said that there are essentially two positions, both clearly unsatisfying, neither of which gives us a real answer.

On the one hand we have a form of a rejection of life in the name of death: I quoted the words of the Greek philosopher Plato. "The life of a righteous man," said he, "is an eternal dying." Here, as in many religions, one finds the irrevocable victory of death, which violates the purpose of life. For if it is inevitable that we must die, then it is best to transfer all our hopes and aspirations to that other, mystical world.

But I call this answer unsatisfactory because it is precisely about this other world that man has no

The Last Enemy

knowledge. And how can we have as the object of our love that about which we know nothing? This is the source of man's reaction against various "funereal," "death-centered" religions, the rejection of pathetic and sorrow-filled worldviews. But while rejecting them in the name of *this* life, in the name of *this* world, man still is not liberated from the oppressive sense of the awareness of death. On the contrary, having lost the perspective of eternity, he becomes even more fragile, even more ephemeral on this earth. As Pasternak wrote:

> We shall stroll through the dwellings
> With flashlights in hand,
> We also shall search,
> And we also shall die.

All of civilization seems to be permeated with a passionate obsession to stifle this fear of death and the sense of the meaninglessness of life that oozes out of it like a slow-dripping poison. What is this intense conflict with religion, if nothing other than a mindless attempt to root out of human consciousness the memory and concern with death and consequently the question: why do I live in this brief and fragile life?

And so we have two answers, neither of which in the final analysis gives us anything. And it is this dilemma that leads us to ask: but what does Christianity say to us about death? Even if we know nothing about Christianity, we cannot help but recall that its attitude toward death is radically different—it can't be reduced to one of the two approaches cited above.

"The last enemy to be destroyed is death." So, it is as if we suddenly find ourselves in a different dimension: death is an enemy that must be destroyed. We find ourselves so removed from Plato and his efforts to force us not only to become used to the idea of death but actually to

The Last Enemy

love this thought and to transform our whole life into an "exercise about death."

Christ weeps at the grave of his dead friend Lazarus—what a powerful witness! He does not say, "Well, now he is in heaven, everything is well; he is separated from this difficult and tormented life." Christ does not say all those things we do in our pathetic and uncomforting attempts to console. In fact he says nothing—he weeps. And then, according to the Gospels, he raises his friend, that is, he restores him into that life from which we are supposedly to find liberation toward a higher good.

Furthermore, is it not a fact that Easter stands at the center of Christianity, with its joyful proclamation that death has been overthrown? "Trampling down death by death!" Did not Christianity enter into and rule the world during many centuries with this unheard-of proclamation: "death is conquered in victory"? Is not

O DEATH, WHERE IS THY STING?

Christianity first of all faith in the resurrection of Christ from the dead, in the assertion that "the dead shall arise and those in the graves shall rejoice"?

Yes, indeed this is all true, yet within Christianity itself and among individual Christians we now find the weakening of this victorious, new, and, from the viewpoint of this world, foolish faith. And Christians have themselves begun to slowly return to Plato, not with his opposition of life and death as two enemies, but in the opposition of two worlds: "this world" and the other world, in which supposedly rejoice all the immortal souls of people who have died.

But Christ never spoke about the immortality of souls—he spoke about the resurrection of the dead! And how can we fail to see that between these two approaches there is an immense abyss? For, surely, if the question is strictly about the immortality of souls, then we need not concern

The Last Enemy

ourselves with death as such, and what need have we of all these words about victory over death, about its destruction, and about resurrection?

"The last enemy to be destroyed is death." And so, let us ask ourselves: in what sense is death the last enemy? Whose enemy is death? And how did this enemy become the ruler of the world and the master of life? We may recall the lines from Vladimir Soloviev's poem: "Death and Time have dominion on earth / you must refrain from calling them lords . . ."[1] But how can we not recognize the lordship of all that has become normal, the rule of life, with which man has long ago come to terms, against which he has ceased to protest and about which he has ceased even to be concerned in his philosophy, the enemy with which he seeks to find a compromise both in his religion and his culture?

Indeed, the Christian teaching about death is no longer heard, and Christians themselves can no longer deal with it, for in essence Christianity is not concerned about coming to terms with death, but rather with the victory over it. And when this subject is discussed with the attitude of the foolish Russian philosopher Fedorov, then immediately it is blindly accepted as the voice of wisdom, the voice of compromise, the voice of inevitability. But if such is the case, then I repeat, the whole Christian faith is meaningless, for the apostle Paul said: "If Christ has not been raised then . . . your faith is in vain" (1 Cor 15:14). So it is to this theme—the Christian understanding of death—that we will return in our next conversation.

---

[1]Vladimir S. Soloviev, *Stikhotvoreniia i shutochnye pesy* (München: Wilhelm Fink Verlag, 1968), p. 93.

CHAPTER 3

The Origin of Death

In my last conversation I referred to the Gospel account in which Christ weeps at the grave of his friend Lazarus. We need to pause and consider the meaning of these tears, for in this very moment there occurs a unique transformation within religion in relation to the long-standing religious approach to death.

I already spoke about the meaning of this transformation. Up to this moment the purpose of religion, as well as the purpose of philosophy, consisted in enabling man to come to terms with death, and if possible even to make death desirable: death as the liberation from the oppressiveness of the body; death as the liberation from suffering; death as freedom from this changing, busy, evil world; death as the beginning of eternity. Here, in fact, is the sum total of religious and philosophical teaching before Christ and outside of Christianity—in primitive religions, in Greek philosophy, in Buddhism, and so forth. But Christ *weeps* at the grave of his friend, and in so doing he reveals his own struggle with death, his refusal to acknowledge it and to come to terms with it. Suddenly, death ceases to be a normal and natural fact, it appears as something foreign, as unnatural, as fearsome

The Origin of Death

and perverted, and it is acknowledged as an enemy: "The last enemy to be destroyed is death."

In order to feel the whole depth and revolutionary force of this change we must begin at the beginning, at the source of this new and unprecedented approach to death. We find it as a brief statement in Holy Scripture: "God did not make death, and he does not delight in the death of the living" (Wis 1:13). This means that in the world, in creation, there is a power that does not have its origin in God, which he did not desire, which he did not create, which opposes him and is independent of him.

God created life. Always and everywhere God is himself called the Life and the giver of life. In that eternally new and eternally childlike story in the Bible, God delights in his world, in its resplendent light and in its joy of life.

To be more precise, and to bring this story revealed in the Bible to its conclusion, one can put it this way: death is the denial of God, and if death is natural, if it is the ultimate truth about life and about the world, if it is the highest and immutable law about all of creation, then there is no God, then this whole story about creation, about joy, and about the light of life is a total lie.

Therefore, the most important and most profound question of the Christian faith must be, How and from where did death arise, and why has it become stronger than life? Why has it become so powerful that the world itself has become a kind of cosmic cemetery, a place where a collection of people condemned to death live either in fear or terror, or in their efforts to forget about death find themselves rushing around one great big burial plot?

To this question Christianity answers with equal force, brevity, and conviction. Here is the text: "and through sin death has come into the world" (Rom 5:12). In other words, for Christianity,

The Origin of Death

death first of all is revealed as part of the moral order, as a spiritual catastrophe. In some final and indescribable sense man *desired death*, or perhaps one might say, he did not desire that life that was given to him by God freely, with love and joy.

Surely it is an indisputable fact that life consists in total interdependence. In the words of Holy Scripture man does not have life in himself. He always receives it from outside, from others, and always depends on the other—for air, for food, for light, for warmth, for water. It is precisely this dependency that materialism emphasizes with such force. And it is justified in doing so, for indeed man is inextricably, naturally, biologically, physiologically dependent on the world.

But whereas materialism sees in this fact the final truth about the world and about humanity (for it regards this determinism as a self-evident rule of nature), Christianity sees here the Fall and the perversion of the world and of humanity. This is what it calls the *original sin*.

The world is a perpetual revelation of God about himself to humanity; it is only a means of communion, of this constant, free, and joyful encounter with the only content of life—with the Life of life itself—with God.

"You have created us for yourself, Lord, and our hearts cannot rest, until they find their rest in You!"[1]

But the tragedy—and herein lies the heart of the Christian teaching about sin—is that man did not desire this life with God and for God. He desired life *for himself*, and in himself he found the purpose, the goal, and the content of life. And in this free choice of himself, and not of God, in his preference for himself over God, without realizing it, man became inextricably a slave of the world, a slave of his own dependence

The Origin of Death

on the world. He eats in order to live, but with his food he communes with what is mortal, for food does not have life in itself.

Feuerbach said, "Man is what he eats." Yes indeed, but what he eats has just died; he eats in order to live, but instead he began living in order to eat, and in this senseless and vicious circle lies the horrible determinism of human life.

Thus, death is the fruit of a life that is poisoned and perpetually disintegrating, a disintegration to which man has freely subjected himself. Not having life in himself, he has subjected himself to the world of death.

"God did not create death." It is man who introduced death into the world, freely desiring life only for himself and in himself, cutting himself off from the source, the goal, and content of life—from God. And this is why death—as disintegration, as separation, as temporality,

O DEATH, WHERE IS THY STING?

transitoriness—has become the supreme law of life, revealing the illusory nature of everything on earth.

In order to console himself, man created a dream of another world where there is no death, and for that dream he forfeited *this* world, gave it up decidedly to death. Only if we fully return to the Christian understanding about death, as the root of man's own perversion of the understanding of the very content of life, can we hear once more, as new, the Christian proclamation about the destruction of death in the resurrection.

---

[1] Augustine, *Confessions*, 1.1.

CHAPTER 4

The Resurrection of the Body

Everything mentioned in our previous discussions now brings us firmly to our main theme, to the heart of Christianity—the proclamation of the resurrection. I wish to emphasize that I am not speaking simply about the immortality of the soul after its separation from the

O DEATH, WHERE IS THY STING?

body, not simply about some kind of mystical bodiless existence in some mysterious ethereal other world. I am speaking precisely about the resurrection.

"The dead shall arise, and those in the graves shall rejoice!" How these words resound! How triumphant, joyous, filled with promise; with what foretaste of the future do these words ring out late in the night of Holy Friday, when already through the darkness and sadness of the grave, of the Cross, and of the shroud there begins to shine this imperceptible light of the approaching Pascha. As that most ancient Christian confession of faith, the so-called Apostle's Creed, so simply affirms: "I believe in the resurrection of the body."

Following Christ's resurrection, when he appeared to the frightened and confused disciples, according to the words of the Gospel, they thought that they had seen an apparition. He

The Resurrection of the Body

said to them: "Do not be afraid . . . it is I, touch me, and be convinced that a ghost does not have a body, as I do." And after this he took food, fish and bread, "and ate before them" (Lk 24:36-43).

The apostles went out from Jerusalem with the message of the resurrection, and they preached the resurrection of the dead to the ends of the earth. And this faith, this joyful news, this proclamation became the joy and the life of those who made the words of the apostles their own.

But for the world of that time, this was an unheard-of and absurd preaching. That world could reluctantly accept the notion of the immortality of souls, but considered the resurrection of the body to be totally ludicrous. When the apostle Paul preached this in Athens, at the very center of Greek wisdom and enlightenment, the philosophers who listened to him laughed, saying to Paul: "We will hear you again about this" (Acts 17:32).

O DEATH, WHERE IS THY STING?

But I am convinced that even now, two thousand years after the founding of Christianity, it is difficult, if not impossible, for humanity to understand this preaching, to understand why Christianity itself stands or falls precisely on this teaching. Indeed, we celebrate Easter, it is indisputable that something happens to us when each year the evening silence is broken with the proclamation, "Christ is risen!" and with its unique response, "Indeed he is risen!" But if at that point we begin contemplating the meaning of all of this, what we are really celebrating on this Easter night, why we are joyful and the meaning of this joy for us, for me, then everything becomes muddled and hard to understand.

The resurrection of the body—what do we really mean by this? Where is it, this body, dissolved in the earth, returned to the mysterious cycle of nature? Are we to think that these bones will arise? And indeed, why do we need a body in that mystical, spiritual other world? Did not the

The Resurrection of the Body

mystics and sages of all times teach us that the positive meaning of death is precisely that it liberates us from the prison of the body, as they say, from this perennial dependency on the material, physical, and bodily life—finally rendering our souls light, weightless, free, spiritual?

Perhaps we can approach this question from a new perspective if we consider more profoundly the meaning of the body. Furthermore, we must not consider this issue abstractly, in purely philosophical terms but, so to say, practically—in other words, we must consider the role of the body in our, in my, life.

On the one hand, of course it is entirely clear that all of our bodies are transitory and impermanent. Biologists have calculated that all the cells that compose our bodies are replaced every seven years. Thus, physiologically, every seven years we have a new body. Therefore, at the end of my life the body that is laid in the grave or

O DEATH, WHERE IS THY STING?

consumed by fire is no longer the same body as all the preceding ones, and in the final analysis each of our bodies is nothing other than our individual incarnation in the world, as the form of my dependence on the world, on the one hand, and of my life and of my activity in the world, on the other.

In essence, my body is my relationship to the world, to others; it is my life as communion and as mutual relationship. Without exception, everything in the body, in the human organism, is created for this relationship, for this communion, for this coming out of oneself. It is not an accident, of course that love, the highest form of communion, finds its incarnation in the body; the body is that which sees, hears, feels, and thereby leads me out of the isolation of my *I*.

But then, perhaps, we can say in response: the body is not the darkness of the soul, but rather the body is its freedom, for the body is the soul

The Resurrection of the Body

as love, the soul as communion, the soul as life, the soul as movement. And this is why, when the soul loses the body, when it is separated from the body, it loses life; it dies, even if this dying of the soul is not a complete annihilation, but a dormition, or sleep.

And so, indeed, every form of sleep, and not only the sleep of death, is a kind of dying of one's organism, for in sleep it is precisely the body that sleeps and is inactive. And here we find no life except one that is suspended, unreal—there is nothing but sleep. If this is the case, then when Christianity speaks about the resurrection of the body, it does not speak about the vivification of bones and muscles, for bones and muscles and the whole material world, its whole fabric, is nothing more than certain basic elements, in the end—atoms. And in them there is nothing specifically personal, nothing eternally mine.

Christianity speaks about the restoration of life

O DEATH, WHERE IS THY STING?

as communion, it speaks about the spiritual body that over the course of our whole life we have developed through love, through our pursuits, through our relationships, through our coming out of ourselves. It speaks not about the eternity of matter, but about its final spiritualization; about the world that finally becomes truly a body—the life and love of mankind; about the world that has become fully communion with Life.

The cult of cemeteries and gravestones is not a Christian cult, for the Christian proclamation is not about the dissolution in nature of some part of matter that served as someone's body, but about the resurrection of life in all its fulness and completion, fulfilled in love.

In this lies the meaning of Easter, here is the final power and joy of Christianity. "Death is swallowed up in victory" (1 Cor 15:54).

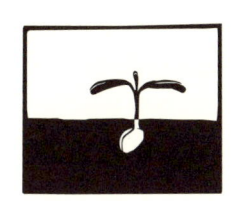

CHAPTER 5

The Week of the Cross

In the middle of Great Lent, at the end of the third week, in every church the cross is brought out into the middle of the temple. The faithful come up to venerate it, and we begin our approach to the most important, most mystical of all the themes

O DEATH, WHERE IS THY STING?

of our faith—the theme of crucifixion, of suffering, and of death.

Why is it mystical? Isn't suffering at the very center of life? Isn't each one of us aware of it all too often? Yes, this is certainly true. But here the question is not about us, but about Christ. And is not our affirmation about Christ that he is God? But is it not also a fact that from God, from faith, we demand comfort (if not the complete annihilation of our sufferings)? Do not the adherents as well as the opponents of faith contend in some odd agreement that religion means first of all help, comfort, a certain balm for the soul, as they say?

Yet here is the cross, which reappears on Holy Friday, and again we hear the same words: "... he began to be sorrowful and troubled" (Mt 26:37), and he said, "My soul is very sorrowful, even to death" (Mt 26:38). Instead of helping his apostles, who are numb with sorrow and despair, he

The Week of the Cross

asks help from them: "Remain here, and watch with me" (Mt 26:38). And then, that lonely suffering: first the assault, then the derision, slapping on the face, spitting, the nails in the hands and feet. And most terrible of all—abandonment. Everyone abandons him, everyone runs away. It is as if the whole sky was hidden, for "about the ninth hour Jesus cried with a loud voice, 'my God, my God, why have you forsaken me?'" (Mt 27:46).

No, if we begin to the truly examine this, if we listen to it carefully, something strange happens here with religion itself. It seems as if nothing familiar remains—no assistance, no support, no guarantee. Put up a candle, offer a service for help or a memorial, and everything in life will be well, God will come to our aid, here as well as there, after a horrible and mysterious death. Is this not the simplified concept of faith that prevails among most believers? Did they not already at the time of Christ follow him in great crowds, hoping for healing, help, and useful teachings? Notice carefully how in the Gospel accounts this crowd gradually diminishes. He is abandoned by that rich young man who thinks that he has observed all the commandments of religion but who in the end is unable to grasp Christ's words: "If you would be perfect, go and sell what you possess and give to the poor, and you will have treasure in heaven; and come, follow me" (Mt 19:21). On the night of the great supper of love, his disciple leaves in order to betray him. And finally, at the end, they all abandon him and flee.

In our life things are exactly reversed: we begin alone, in obscurity, and then come acknowledgment and accolades, a host of admirers. In the Gospel, however, when things end at the Cross, Christ remains alone. Furthermore, he says about the coming time: "They have persecuted me, they will persecute you" (Jn 15:20), "In the world you have tribulation" (Jn 16:33). And there is only one vocation given to us, only one

The Week of the Cross

requirement—to pick up our cross and to carry it, and we already know what this cross is.

Indeed, something strange happens here with religion: instead of help, we are given the cross, instead of promises of comfort and well-being, we hear the certainty: "They persecuted me, they will persecute you." And when we hear the Gospel about the Pharisees who derided the crucified Christ—"He saved others, he cannot save himself! He is the king of Israel; let him come down now from the cross and we will believe in him" (Mt 27:42)—are we not immediately reminded of the derision and accusations that are heard today: "So, wasn't your God able to help you?"

And indeed, as long as we expect from God only this type of help, only miracles that would eliminate the sufferings from our life, then these accusations will continue. And they will continue because any cheap pill is certainly better

O DEATH, WHERE IS THY STING?

able to relieve a headache than prayer and religion. And we will never understand the mystery of the Cross as long as we expect this type of pill from religion—be it for something trivial or important. As long as this is the case, regardless of all the gold or silver with which it is covered, the Cross remains what the apostle Paul said at the dawn of Christianity: "a scandal for the Jews, and folly for the Gentiles" (1 Cor 1:23). In our given situation the "Jews" represent those who seek only help from religion, while the "Gentiles" are those who seek clever and easy explanations. And in this case the Cross is truly a scandal and folly.

Again the cross is brought out in procession, and that unique week of weeks approaches when the Church invites us not so much to examine and to discuss, but to silently and intensely follow each step of Christ, to follow his slow and irreversible path to suffering, to crucifixion, and to death. It invites us to pick up this very cross.

The Week of the Cross

And something strange happens to us. Suddenly from our own problems, from our own difficulties, and even from our own sufferings we turn our attention to Another, to this silently sorrowful and suffering Person, to this night of horror, betrayal, and loneliness, but also of celebration, of love, and of victory.

Something strange happens to us: perhaps without even knowing it one begins to feel how this cheap and egotistical religion, a religion once demanding only something for itself, demanding that even God would be in its service, evaporates! And it becomes clear, spiritually clear, that at its depths religion is entirely about something else. That in the end it is not all about comfort or help, but about joy and victory.

Thus, in our next talks let us at least mentally follow Christ on this path, as he bears his cross on the way to Golgotha, and perhaps something eternal and eternally important will be once

O DEATH, WHERE IS THY STING?

more revealed to us, to our souls. Here is why in the middle of Lent the cross is brought to the center of the church. This is to what the Church calls us in the so-called week of the Veneration of the Cross, in order that we might begin our own personal movement toward the ultimate, and perhaps the most terrifying, but in the last analysis, the most joyful mystery of our faith.

CHAPTER 6

Pascha[1]

"Christ is risen!—Indeed he is risen!" "Pascha, the Pascha of the Lord, the Feast of feasts, Holy Day of holy days!"[2] What other words can we possibly need? Indeed, "Let no one today lament his poverty, for the Kingdom has come among us."[3]

O DEATH, WHERE IS THY STING?

Yet, no sooner do we hear these amazing words, rejoice in them, believe in them, when suddenly comes the realization that during this festal night, on this radiant day, in fact millions of people do not hear and possibly have never heard them. For so many people these words announce nothing, proclaim nothing. And how many, upon hearing these words, shrug their shoulders in hostility, skepticism, and cynicism? How is it possible to rejoice when so many people do not know this joy, turn away from it, and close their hearts to it? And how is it possible to explain those words and move the hearts of such persons? Again, how can we possibly prove anything to them? About such people Christ said, "even if someone were to return from the dead they would not believe" (Lk 16:31). What can we hope to achieve with our impoverished proofs? Yet, possibly, the full triumphant power of Easter consists precisely in the fact that there is nothing here to prove, that all of man's knowledge, all human proofs are totally powerless before this reality.

Pascha

At the end of the nineteenth century in the very heart of Russia, in a priestly family, we find a young boy named Sergei, "*Seriozha*," Bulgakov. He grows up captivated by the poetry and beauty of church services, with a simple, blind, direct faith. No questions, no proofs. "They didn't even occur to us," he wrote later on, "nor could they occur . . . in us children, given the extent to which we were saturated by this festive life, the extent to which we *loved* the temple and the beauty of its services. How rich and profound and pure was our childhood, how our souls bathed in these heavenly rays that constantly shone on them."[4]

But then came the time of proofs and questioning. And out of this naïve and simple childhood this honest, fervent, and sincere Russian boy fell into the hands of unbelief and atheism, into the world of pure proofs and intellectualism. Seriozha Bulgakov, the son of a humble cemetery priest, became Professor Sergei Nikolayevich

O DEATH, WHERE IS THY STING?

Bulgakov, one of the leaders of the progressive Russian revolutionary intelligentsia, Russian scientific Marxism. Germany, university, friendship with the leaders of Marxism, first scientific works, political economy, glory, and honor—according to the popular phrase—before the whole of thinking Russia. If anyone struggled through that whole process of questioning and proofs, it was certainly he. If anyone achieved all scientific knowledge and its crown and glory in Marxism, then it was surely he. If there was anyone who rejected simple and irresponsible faith, then it was he again. Several years of academic glory, several voluminous books, hundreds of followers. But gradually, one after another all of these proofs began to fall apart and turn into dust, until nothing remained where they once stood. What happened to him—sickness, insanity, grief? No, nothing happened in the external circumstances of his life. What happened is that his soul, the very heart of his consciousness, ceased to accept these flat questions and equally

Pascha

flat answers. The questions ceased to be legitimate questions, the answers ceased to be actual answers. It suddenly became clear that all of this accumulated knowledge failed to answer anything—markets, capital, surplus value . . . what do they know and what can they possibly tell us about the human soul, about its perennial thirst, about that unquenchable desire which, at the deepest level, in its deepest recesses, can never be satisfied?

And so began a return to the sources. Not the reclaiming of a simple naïve childhood faith, not a return to a nostalgic childhood. No, Sergei Bulgakov remained for his whole life an intellectual, a professor, a philosopher, only now his books began to declare something else, his inspired words began to proclaim a different reality.

I remembered him during today's Paschal joy, because it seems to me that with his whole life and with his whole experience he was more

O DEATH, WHERE IS THY STING?

capable than most to answer the question: what proof can one offer? For suddenly this whole question is removed, because he of all people understood the powerlessness and the inefficacy of all of these proofs. He became convinced that Easter is not found in them, nor does it derive its power from them.[5]

Let us hear his words on the day of Pascha near the end of his life: "When the doors are opened, and we enter the temple shining with gleaming lights, during the singing of that exalted Paschal Canon, our hearts are filled with an abundant joy, for Christ has risen from the dead. At that moment a Paschal miracle occurs in our hearts. For we behold Christ's resurrection; we look at the radiant Christ and approach him, the Bridegroom, coming from the grave. We then lose awareness of our surroundings, we seem to come out of ourselves; in the silence of arrested time and the glow of the pure whiteness of Pascha all earthly colors fade, and our soul is

Pascha

smitten solely with the ineffable light of the resurrection. 'Now all is filled with light, heaven and earth, and the regions below.' In the Paschal night mankind is offered a foretaste of the age to come, the possibility of entering the kingdom of glory, the kingdom of God. The language of our world has no words to express this revelation of the Paschal night, its perfect joy. Pascha is life eternal, consisting in being led by God and communion with him. It is truth, peace, and joy in the Holy Spirit. This was the first word with which the resurrected Lord greeted the women disciples: 'rejoice' (Mt 28:9); and greeting him, the first words heard by the apostles were: 'Peace be with you' (Lk 24:36)."

I emphasize, these words of Bulgakov are not the words of a child, the words of a simpleton, who has not yet reached the level of questions and proofs. They are the words of one who speaks *after* all questions have been asked, *after* all proofs given. This is not the proof of Pascha, this is the light, the power, and the victory of Pascha itself within man.

This is why there is nothing for us to prove on this radiant and joyful night. From the very fulness of this joy, of this knowledge, we can only proclaim to the whole world, to those who are near and to those far off: "Christ is risen! Indeed, Christ is risen!"

[1] Dedicated to the memory of Fr Sergius Bulgakov.
[2] Irmos of the Paschal Canon, first ode.
[3] The Paschal Homily of St John Chrysostom.
[4] Fr Sergei Bulgakov, *My Homeland*, autobiographical sketches (posthumous edition) (Paris, 1946) 16.

Pascha

[5] See Fr Alexander's remembrances of Fr Sergei, in honor of the centennial of Fr S.N. Bulgakov's birth, and dedicated to those "extraordinary, and apparently and honorable 'Russian boys,' who there, in Russia, in the stifling Soviet atmosphere, took upon themselves the real feat of resurrecting the Russian spiritual traditions, the return to a profound Russia: for I was also one of those 'Russian boys,' only an immigrant. And this means that I was also, although in a different way, a *stranger* to the circumstances around me, also destined to seek *my own*: that which enabled one to live profoundly, that to which one could truly give oneself, in which one could truly find oneself. But what did I receive at that time from Fr Sergei? He gave us that unique fire that alone is capable of igniting another flame. He let us feel that it is only here where one makes contact with God's light, with the search for it and its comprehension—here was the unique and profound destiny of man, that 'glory of the most exalted vocation,' to which he is called and predestined. He embraced us with his own passion and exultant spirit, with his faith and joy. He brought me into communion with something of the very best and the most pure in the spiritual truth of Russia. And I am convinced that he continues to give the same, to those who open his works even now." Alexander Schmemann, "Tri obraza" [Three Images], in *Vestnik RSKhD (le Messager)*, no. 101-102, 1971: III-IV, p. 11.

CHAPTER 7

The Week of Anti-Pascha (Thomas Sunday)

Thomas, the disciple of Christ, did not believe the other disciples when they told him that they had seen the resurrected Teacher. "If I do not see in his hands the prints of the nails, and if I do not place my hand in the wounds of those nails, if I

O DEATH, WHERE IS THY STING?

do not place my hand in his side, I will not believe" (Jn 20:25). And, of course, this is the same sentiment expressed by mankind through all ages.

Is not all knowledge and science based on these words—I will see, I will touch, I will believe? Is this not the foundation on which people build all their theories and ideologies? And it seems that Christ not only asks us the impossible, but something seemingly untrue and wrong: "Blessed are those who have not seen," he says, "and yet believe" (Jn 20:29). But how is it possible not to see and still to believe? And in what? Not simply to believe in the existence of some kind of higher spiritual being, in God, not simply in goodness, in justice, or in humanity—no. But to believe in the resurrection of the dead—in the unprecedented and mind-boggling proclamation that lies at the heart of Christianity: "Christ is risen!"

The Week of Anti-Pascha

Where must this faith come from? Can we *force* ourselves to believe?

And so, with sadness or in anger people abandon this impossible call and return to their simple and clear affirmations—to see, to touch, to feel, to prove. But strangely enough, no matter how much man looks or verifies or touches, that final truth that he is seeking remains mysterious and continues to elude him.

He thinks that he has finally achieved justice, and then it is suddenly gone—he finds the same decline, domination, tyranny, and lies.

Freedom ... where is it? Before our very eyes, the very same people who affirmed that they have found the most genuine, universal, scientific happiness have sent millions of people to concentration camps in the name of their happiness, justice, and freedom. And the horrible fear continues not to diminish but to increase, and

O DEATH, WHERE IS THY STING?

hatred along with it. Instead of diminishing, sadness increases. They have seen it all, they have checked it all, touched it, calculated everything, analyzed everything, and in their scientific laboratories and offices evolved the most advanced and proven theory of happiness. Yet it turns out that it results not in the slightest, most simple, most basic earthly happiness, that it fails to give the most simple, direct, and living joy, but rather keeps demanding more sacrifices, new sufferings and swells the ocean of hatred, persecution, and evil.

And yet after many centuries Easter continues to evoke this happiness and joy—here where it would seem that nothing can be seen or verified, where nothing can be examined. Yet, no sooner do we arrive at church on Easter night and look into the faces illuminated by the flickering candles than we immediately enter this anticipation, we sense the slow yet certain mounting joy.

The Week of Anti-Pascha

In the darkness we hear the first "Christ is risen!" and thousands of voices reply: "Indeed he is risen!" The doors of the temple are opened, the light emerges, and we begin to feel the slow igniting and increase of that incomparable joy that can never be experienced except here in this moment. "Exult and be glad . . ." Where do these words come from, from where is this cry, this triumph of happiness, from where comes this certain knowledge? Truly, "Blessed are those who have not seen and still believe." But it is precisely here that it is shown and proven. Come, touch, verify, and feel, you also, O you skeptics, weak in faith and blind guides of the blind!

The Church refers to the hesitant apostle as "Doubting Thomas," the unbeliever, and it is significant that it commemorates him specifically the first week after Pascha, calling it "Thomas Sunday." For of course, it reminds us not only about Thomas, but about each person, about humanity. My Lord, what a desert of fear, of mindlessness,

O DEATH, WHERE IS THY STING?

and of suffering has mankind produced with all of its progress and all of its synthetic happiness! It has reached the moon, it has overcome distances, has conquered nature, yet it seems that no words of Holy Scripture so well express the state of the world as: "the whole creation has been groaning in travail" (Rom 8:22). It truly groans and suffers, and in the midst of the suffering resounds that proud and senseless and fearful declaration: "If I do not see, I will not believe."

But Christ had pity on Thomas and came to him and said: "Put your finger here, and see my hands; and put out your hand and place it in my side; do not be faithless, but believing" (Jn 20:27). And Thomas fell before him on his knees and exclaimed: "My Lord and my God!" (Jn 20:28). It was the end of his pride, his self-assurance, his self-satisfaction: I am not gullible like all of you, you can't fool me. He yielded, he believed, he gave himself—and in that instant he achieved that freedom, that happiness and joy,

The Week of Anti-Pascha

those very things for which he refused simply to believe, expecting proofs.

During the Paschal days we have before us two images, the risen Christ and the unbelieving Thomas: from One emanates joy and happiness, while from the other agony and unbelief. Which one will we choose, to which one will we go, which one of the two will we believe? In the course of the whole of human history we receive from One that never-fading ray of Paschal light, Paschal joy, while from the other, that dark agony of unbelief and doubt...

In essence, today we can verify it, we can touch it and we can see it, for this joy is among us now. But the suffering is there also. What will we choose, what will we desire, what will we *see*? Perhaps it is not too late to exclaim not only with our voices, but truly with our whole being, that which the unbelieving Thomas exclaimed when he finally saw: "My Lord and my God!"

CHAPTER 8

The Nature of Man

One of the popular critiques of Christianity relates to its teaching about the fall of man. In this teaching the opponents of Christianity see a pessimistic attitude and the demeaning of human dignity. Perhaps in light of what I was discussing previously this accusation begins to lose its demagogic sting.

O DEATH, WHERE IS THY STING?

I began my conversations by citing Feuerbach, one of the founders of contemporary materialism. Feuerbach is remembered for his classic statement: "Man is what he eats." Ironically, in this seeming reduction of humanity to food, to matter, without realizing it, Feuerbach himself said exactly what the Bible says about mankind. The Bible teaches us that man is first of all a being who is thirsty and hungry, who transforms the world into his own life. But in contrast to Feuerbach, who subjects humanity to food and matter, the Bible sees in this transformation the goal of humanity to make the world into life, and thereby make it a means of communion with the world, with its beginnings, with its purpose, with God. I said that in return for God's gift to man—the gift of the world, of food, of life—man responds with thanksgiving and praise, with which he fills and transfigures the world. Only in light of this basic biblical teaching can we understand why the symbol of man's fall in the Bible is also connected with food.

The Nature of Man

On the basis of the mythical (that is, symbolic) story in the Bible, the whole world was given by God as food to man, with the exception of one forbidden fruit. And it is precisely this fruit that man eats, refusing to believe and to obey God.

What is the meaning of this story, which greets us like a child's fable? It means that the fruit of this one tree, in contrast to all others, was not given as a *gift* to man. It did not bear God's blessing. This means that if man ate this fruit, he did not eat it in order to have life with God, as a means of transforming it into life, but rather as a goal in itself, and thus, having consumed it, man subjected himself to food. He desired to have life not from God or for God but rather for himself.

The very fall of man consists in the fact that he desired life for himself and in himself, and not for God and in God. God made this very world a means of communion with himself, but man desired the world purely for himself alone.

O DEATH, WHERE IS THY STING?

Instead of returning God's love with love for him, man fell in love with the world, as a goal in itself. But herein lies the whole problem, that the world cannot be an end in and of itself, just as food has no purpose unless it is transformed into life. So too, the world, having ceased to be transparent to God, has become an endless commotion, a senseless cycle of time in which everything is constantly in flux, constantly vanishing, and, in the final analysis, dying.

In the divine conception of humanity, dependence on the world was overcome by the transformation of the world itself into life. Life means possessing God. "In him was life, and the life was the light of men"—so we read in the Gospel of John (1:4). But if the world is no longer transformed into anything, if life ceases to be a transformation into communion with Absolute Meaning, with Absolute Beauty, with Absolute Goodness, then this world becomes not only meaningless, it becomes *death*. Nothing

The Nature of Man

has life in and by itself, everything vanishes, everything dissolves. Cut off from its roots, a flower can live for a short time in water and even decorate a room, but we realize that it is dying, that it is already subject to corruption.

Man ate the forbidden fruit, thinking that it would give him life. But life itself outside of and without God is simply communion with death. It is no accident that what we eat already needs to be dead in order to become our life. We eat in order to live, but since we eat something that is already deprived of life, food itself inevitably leads us to death. And in death there neither is nor can be any life.

"Man is what he eats." There it is, he eats . . . death—dead animals, dead vegetation, rot and dissolution. He himself dies and, perhaps, the enormity of his fall consists precisely in the fact that this very death-filled and corrupt life, this life defined from the very beginning by corruption, this life that flows and irrevocably vanishes—this life he considers absolutely normal. And he is confirmed in this attitude by those who dare to blame Christianity as being pessimistic and as destructive toward man. But when Christ approached the grave of his friend Lazarus, and they said to him, "Do not come near, for he already stinks" (Jn 11:39), Christ did not consider this normal—he wept.

"I am the image of your ineffable glory"[1]—and yet they remove him and hide him so that he would not smell and disrupt their routines—this Man, this image and likeness of God, this king and crown of creation! Indeed, this horrible meaninglessness of the world, this constant commotion of mankind within a cosmic cemetery, these pathetic attempts to build something for those who are dying, for those already dead, and finally, the affirmation of all of this as normal and natural—this is what Christianity declares as the Fall, as the falsification by man of

The Nature of Man

himself and of his divine and eternal calling. It refuses to come to terms with such a worldview, and firmly and clearly proclaims: "The last enemy to be destroyed is death" (1 Cor 15:26).

We began these conversations with food, with Feuerbach's "man is what he eats." At the same time we saw that Christianity also places the fundamental hunger of mankind at the center of its understanding. However, Christianity alone offers an entirely unique approach to the question of what man is ultimately seeking, of what is the *only* thing that can satisfy his hunger. *What* is it that he desires? Feuerbach and the rest of the materialists will answer: he wants freedom, he wants prosperity, and he wants to be well fed. But what is the use of freedom, prosperity, and food to one who is condemned to death? Why should one build vacation homes in a cemetery? Whatever we pursue, everything ends up in this dead-end, which Vladimir Soloviev described so well: "death and time are reigning on earth . . ."

O DEATH, WHERE IS THY STING?

To this question Christianity answers: man desires life, not simply for a moment, but for eternity, life which in the church's hymnography so beautifully is called "life unfading." This life is not to be found in food, although it is through food that man receives it, and not in the air, although breathing gives him the possibility to search for and desire it, and not even in good health. This life is in the One who is himself Life, that is, in God—in the knowledge of him, in communion with him, in love and in praise and in the possession of him. This is why it is the one who is fallen into death and into servitude to food, having become only that which he eats—this man—who needs to be saved. Subsequently, this becomes the basic theme of Christianity, the teaching about salvation, about the restoration and resurrection of man from death to Life.

---

[1] Hymn from the Orthodox funeral service.

CHAPTER 9

The Religion of Salvation

We affirm that Christianity is the religion of salvation. But what is it a salvation *from*, and how is this salvation accomplished? Sadly, it is Christians themselves who have so often oversimplified, darkened, and distorted the concept of salvation, providing the

O DEATH, WHERE IS THY STING?

very ammunition for the comparable simplifications and distortions of the opponents of religion.

"Christians are insignificant and weak people who need salvation; we, on the other hand, have no need for salvation, we will save ourselves"; "in the great struggle you will establish your own rights"—and to this we can add—"salvation"... These and similar retorts are hurled at Christianity by antireligionists. This is why it is essential and fundamental for us to understand what in the biblical language and in the language of Christianity is the meaning of the term salvation. But this is possible only in light of our previous conversations about the fall of man. For the whole point, of course, is not about salvation from some misfortunes or accidents, from illnesses, from various sufferings, and so forth. It would seem that this should be self-evident even to Christians themselves, who often seek in their religion precisely this superficial help, as a kind

The Religion of Salvation

of additional insurance. We must maintain unequivocally that such an understanding about salvation is perverse and distorted. This is evident first of all in the account of that terrible night before his betrayal and death, when Christ is alone in the garden, abandoned by his sleeping disciples. He is praying that this cup would pass, and in the Gospel we read that he "began to be greatly distressed and troubled" (Mk 14:33).

If indeed Christianity is supposed to be a religion of salvation from earthly evils and tribulations then it is certainly a total failure.

No, it is not with this kind of salvation that we are concerned. We are concerned rather with that salvation of which we spoke previously, from that radical and tragic transformation that occurred and is still constantly taking place in the rapport of man with his own life—a transformation that man himself is already incapable of correcting and restoring. The name that I gave

O DEATH, WHERE IS THY STING?

to this transformation, to this fall, is death; death, not only as the end of life, but life itself as a senseless waste, as diminution and disappearance, life itself as a dying, already from the moment of birth; the transformation of the world into a cosmic cemetery; the hopeless subjection of man to disintegration, to time, and to death. It is not the weak person but rather the one who is strong who seeks salvation, who thirsts for it. The weak person looks for help. The weak person desires that mediocre and boring happiness that is offered to him by the various ideologues that have once and for all come to terms with death. The weak ones are content to accept to live for a while and then to die. Those who are strong consider such a view unworthy of man and of the world. This is our response to the opponents of Christianity who claim that we are terribly weak if we need salvation. It is not we alone who need this, but that whole image of the world and of the true life that lives in man; that whole being, which recoils

The Religion of Salvation

against this senseless commotion on a globe stuffed with corpses.

Therefore, the Christian understanding of salvation means a restoration of that life, Life with a capital "L," Life eternal and unfading, for which man knows he is created. And it is not a sign of his weakness but rather of his strength that man hungers for salvation and receives it from God. For God is that very Life that man had lost, subjecting himself irrevocably to the world, having lost himself completely in time and in death. And so we believe and we know, as John the Evangelist says: "Life was made manifest" (1 Jn 1:2).

God did not save us by the exercise of power, nor with a miracle, nor by force or through fear, nor by intimidation, but only by coming among us in the world and for the world, for life itself—life as divine beauty, as wisdom, and as goodness, life as the beauty of the world and of man, life as

O DEATH, WHERE IS THY STING?

capable in itself and by itself to transform, to obliterate, and to consume death. And this Life appeared not as one more philosophical theory, not as a principal of organization, but as a Person. Yes, Christianity teaches and proclaims that in one Person, in one place, and at one point in time, Divine Life appeared to mankind in the image of the perfect Man—Jesus Christ from Nazareth in Galilee.

The intellectual, the technocrat, the so-called "contemporary man" shrugs his shoulders and declares: what nonsense! And yes, nonsense or not, it is this image, this Person, this Life, which over the course of two thousand years has held an incomparable sway over the hearts and lives of people. There is no single teaching, no philosophy, which has not changed or vanished over time; not one kingdom, not one culture, which has not faded into history. But if there was and if there is in history a miracle, it is the memory of this one Person, who did not write a single line,

The Religion of Salvation

who was in no way concerned with what would be said about him later on—a Person who died a shameful death on a cross, as a criminal, a Person who lives, truly lives, in those who believe in him. He said of himself, "I am the way, and the truth, and the life" (Jn 14:6). Now millions of people walk along this way, preserve this truth, live by this life, so that even the most powerful government, which precisely organizes every detail of people's lives from cradle to grave, controlling each word, each thought, each breath—even that government—is powerless before this faith.

Christ is the savior of the world—this is the most ancient Christian affirmation. And he saved the world and us by virtue of giving us the possibility to live life independently of death and time, and in this lies our salvation. If the apostle Paul accepted Christ after a long period of persecuting his disciples and suddenly exclaimed, "For me to live is Christ, and to die is gain!" (Phil 1:21),

O DEATH, WHERE IS THY STING?

then we can certainly say that something has radically changed in the world.

Indeed, people continue dying as they did before, and the world continues to be filled with separations, with sadness and suffering. But within that world there has been ignited and continues to burn the light of faith. It is not simply a belief that somewhere, at some point beyond the confines of this life, our existence will continue—this idea existed even before Christ. But in the fact that the world itself and life itself have once more received purpose and meaning, that time itself has become filled with light, that eternity has entered into our life already here and now. Eternity is first of all the knowledge of God, which is open to us through Christ. There is no more loneliness, there is no more fear and darkness. I am with you, says Christ, I am with you now and always, with complete love, with all knowledge, with all power. Eternity is the commandment of love

The Religion of Salvation

that Christ left us. "By this all men will know that you are my disciples, if you have love for one another" (Jn 13:35). And finally the name of this eternity is "peace and joy in the Holy Spirit" (Rom 14:17), and of this joy Christ says, "no one will take your joy from you" (Jn 16: 22). Salvation is nothing less than all of this.

APPENDIX

Trampling Down Death by Death

We live today in a death-denying culture. This can clearly be seen in the unobtrusive appearance of the ordinary funeral home, in its attempt to look like all other houses. Inside, the "funeral director" tries to take care of things in such a way that

O DEATH, WHERE IS THY STING?

one will not notice that one is sad; and a parlor ritual is designed to transform a funeral into a semi-pleasant experience. There is a strange conspiracy of silence concerning the blunt fact of death, and the corpse itself is "beautified" so as to disguise its deadness. But there existed in the past and there still exist—even within our life-affirming modern world—"death-centered" cultures, in which death is the one great all-embracing preoccupation, and life itself is conceived as being mainly preparation for death. If to some the funeral home itself seems to divert thoughts from death, to some others even the "utilities" such as a bed or a table become symbols, reminders of death. A bed is seen as the image of the grave, the casket is put on the table.

Where is Christianity in all this? There can be no doubt, on the one hand, that the "problem of death" is central and essential in its message, which announces Christ's victory over death,

Trampling Down Death by Death

and that Christianity has its source in that victory. Yet, on the other hand, one has the strange feeling that although this message has certainly been heard, it has had no real impact on the basic human attitudes toward death. It is rather Christianity that has "adjusted" itself to these attitudes, accepted them as its own. It is not difficult to dedicate to God—in a nice Christian sermon—new skyscrapers and world's fairs, to join—if not to lead—the great progressive and life-affirming forces of our "atomic age," to make Christianity appear as the very source of all this hectic and life-centered activity. And it is equally easy, when preaching at a funeral or a retreat, to present life as a valley of suffering and vanity, and to present death as a liberation.

A Christian minister, representative in this of the whole Church, must today use *both languages*, espouse both attitudes. But if he is sincere, he must inescapably feel that "something is missing" in both, and that this is in fact *the Christian element itself.* For it falsifies the Christian message to present and to preach Christianity as essentially life-affirming—without referring this affirmation to the death of Christ and therefore to the very fact of death; and to pass over in silence the fact that for Christianity, death is not only the end, but indeed the very reality of *this world*. But to "comfort" people and reconcile them with death by making this world a meaningless scene of an individual preparation for death is also to falsify it. For Christianity proclaims that Christ died for the life of the world, and not for an "eternal rest" from it. This "falsification" makes the very success of Christianity (according to official data, church building and per capita contributions to churches have reached an all time high!) into a profound tragedy. The worldly man wants the minister to be an optimistic fellow, sanctioning faith in an optimistic and progressive world. And the religious man sees him as an utterly serious, sadly solemn, and dignified denouncer of the world's vanity and

Trampling Down Death by Death

futility. The world does not want religion and religion does not want Christianity. The one rejects death, the other, life. Hence the immense frustration either with the secularistic tendencies of the life-affirming world or with the morbid religiosity of those who oppose it.

This frustration will last as long as Christians continue to understand Christianity as a religion whose purpose is to *help*, as long as they continue to keep the "utilitarian" self-consciousness typical of the "old religion." For this was, indeed, one of the main functions of religions: to help, and especially to help people to die. For this reason religion has always been an attempt to *explain* death, and by explaining it, to reconcile man with it. What pains Plato took in his *Phaedo* to make death desirable and even good, and how often he has since been echoed in the history of human belief when confronted with the prospect of release from this world of change and suffering! Men have consoled themselves with the

O DEATH, WHERE IS THY STING?

rationalization that God made death and that it is therefore right, or with the fact that death belongs to the pattern of life; they have found various meanings in death, or assured themselves that death is preferable to decrepit old age; they have formulated doctrines of the immortality of the soul—that if a man dies, at least a part of him survives. All this has been one long attempt to take the awful uniqueness out of the experience of death.

Christianity, because it is a *religion*, had to accept this fundamental function of religion: to "justify" death and thus to *help*. In doing so, moreover, it more or less assimilated the old and classical explanations of death, common to virtually all religions. For neither the doctrine of the immortality of the soul, based on the opposition between the spiritual and the material, nor that of death as liberation, nor of death as punishment, are, in fact, Christian doctrines. And their integration into the Christian world

Trampling Down Death by Death

view vitiated rather than clarified Christian theology and piety. They "worked" as long as Christianity lived in a "religious" (i.e., death-centered) world. But they ceased to work as soon as the world outgrew this old death-centered religion and became "secular." Yet the world has become secular not because it has become "irreligious," "materialistic," "superficial," not because it has "lost religion"— as so many Christians still think —but because old explanations do not really explain. Christians often do not realize that they themselves, or rather Christianity, has been a major factor in this liberation from the old religion. Christianity, with its message offering fulness of life, has contributed more than anything else to the liberation of man from the fears and the pessimism of religion. Secularism, in this sense, is a phenomenon within the Christian world, a phenomenon impossible without Christianity. Secularism rejects Christianity insofar as Christianity has identified itself with the "old religion" and is forcing upon the world

O DEATH, WHERE IS THY STING?

those "explanations" and "doctrines" of death and life which Christianity has itself destroyed.

It would be a great mistake, however, to think of secularism as simply an "absence of religion." It is, in fact, itself a religion, and as such, an explanation of death and a reconciliation with it. It is the religion of those who are tired of having the world explained in terms of an "other world" of which no one knows anything, and life explained in terms of a "survival" about which no one has the slightest idea; tired of having, in other words, life given "value" in terms of death. Secularism is an "explanation" of death in terms of life. The only world we know is this world, the only life given to us is this life—so thinks a secularist—and it is up to us men to make it as meaningful, as rich, as happy as possible. Life ends with death. This is unpleasant, but since it is natural, since death is a universal phenomenon, the best thing man can do about it is simply to accept it as something natural. As long as

Trampling Down Death by Death

he lives, however, he need not think about it, but should live as though death did not exist. The best way to forget about death is to be busy, to be useful, to be dedicated to great and noble things, to build an always better world. If God exists (and a great many secularists firmly believe in God and the usefulness of religion for their corporate and individual enterprises) and if he, in his love and mercy (for we all have our shortcomings) wants to reward us for our busy, useful, and righteous life with eternal vacations, traditionally called "immortality," it is strictly his gracious business. But immortality is an appendix (however eternal) to this life, in which all real interests, all true values are to be found. The American "funeral home" is indeed the very symbol of secularist religion, for it expresses both the quiet acceptance of death as something natural (a house among other houses with nothing typical about it) and the denial of death's *presence* in life.

O DEATH, WHERE IS THY STING?

Secularism is a religion because it has a faith, it has its own eschatology and its own ethics. And it "works" and it "helps." Quite frankly, if "help" were the criterion, one would have to admit that life-centered secularism *helps* actually more than religion. To compete with it, religion has to present itself as "adjustment to life," "counselling," "enrichment," it has to be publicized in subways and buses as a valuable addition to "your friendly bank" and all other "friendly dealers": try it, it *helps*! And the religious success of secularism is so great that it leads some Christian theologians to "give up" the very category of "transcendence," or in much simpler words, the very idea of "God." This is the price we must pay if we want to be "understood" and "accepted" by modern man, proclaim the Gnostics of the twentieth century.

But it is here that we reach the heart of the matter. For Christianity, *help* is not the criterion. Truth is the criterion. The purpose of Christianity is not to help people by reconciling them with

Trampling Down Death by Death

death, but to reveal the Truth about life and death in order that people may be saved by this Truth. Salvation, however, is not only not identical with help, but is, in fact, opposed to it. Christianity quarrels with religion and secularism not because they offer "insufficient help," but precisely because they "suffice," because they "satisfy" the needs of men. If the purpose of Christianity were to take away from man the fear of death, to reconcile him with death, there would be no need for Christianity, for other religions have done this, indeed, better than Christianity. And secularism is about to produce men who will gladly and corporately die—and not just live—for the triumph of the Cause, whatever it may be.

Christianity is not reconciliation with death. It is the revelation of death, and it reveals death because it is the revelation of Life. Christ is this Life. And only if Christ is Life, is death what Christianity proclaims it to be, namely the enemy

O DEATH, WHERE IS THY STING?

to be destroyed, and not a "mystery" to be explained. Religion and secularism, by explaining death, give it a "status," a rationale, make it "normal." Only Christianity proclaims it to be *abnormal* and, therefore, truly horrible. At the grave of Lazarus Christ wept, and when his own hour to die approached, "he began to be sore amazed and very heavy." In the light of Christ, *this* world, this *life* are lost and are beyond mere "help," not because there is fear of death in them, but because they have accepted and normalized death. To accept God's world as a cosmic cemetery which is to be abolished and replaced by an "other world" which looks like a cemetery ("eternal rest") and to call this religion, to live in a cosmic cemetery and to "dispose" every day of thousands of corpses and to get excited about a "just society" and to be happy!—this is the fall of man. It is not the immorality or the crimes of man that reveal him as a fallen being; it is his "positive ideal"—religious or secular—and his satisfaction with this ideal.

Trampling Down Death by Death

This fall, however, can be truly revealed only by Christ, because only in Christ is the *fulness of life* revealed to us, and death, therefore, becomes "awful," the very fall from life, the enemy. It is *this world* (and not any "other world"), it is *this life* (and not some "other life") that were given to man to be a sacrament of the divine presence given as communion with God, and it is only through this world, this life, by "transforming" them into communion with God that man *was to be*. The horror of death is, therefore, not in its being the "end" and not in physical destruction. By being separation from the world and life, it is *separation from God*. The dead cannot glorify God. It is, in other words, when Christ reveals Life to us that we can hear the Christian message about death as the enemy of God. It is when Life weeps at the grave of the friend, when it contemplates the horror of death, that the victory over death begins.

O DEATH, WHERE IS THY STING?

* * *

Before death, however, there is *dying*: the growth of death in us by physical decay and illness. Here again the Christian approach cannot be simply identified either with that of the modern world, or with the one that characterizes "religion." For the modern secular world, health is the only *normal* state of man; disease therefore is to be fought, and the modern world fights it very well indeed. Hospitals and medicine are among its best achievements. Yet health has a limit, and it is death. There comes a time when the "resources of science" are exhausted—and this the modern world accepts as simply, as lucidly as it accepts death itself. There comes a moment when the patient is to be surrendered to death, to be removed from the ward, and this is done quietly, properly, hygienically—as part of the general routine. As long as a man is alive, everything is to be done to keep him alive, and even if his case is hopeless, it must not be revealed to him. Death

Trampling Down Death by Death

must never be part of life. And although everyone knows that people die in hospitals, their general tone and ethos are those of cheerful optimism. The object of modern medicine's efficient care is life, and not mortal life.

The religious outlook considers disease rather than health to be the "normal" state of man. In this world of mortal and changing matter suffering, sickness, and sorrow are the normal conditions of life. Hospitals and medical care must be supplied, but as a religious duty and not because of any real interest in health as such. Health and healing are always thought of as the mercy of God, from the religious point of view, and real healing is "miraculous." And this miracle is performed by God, again not because health is good, but because it "proves" the power of God and brings men back to God.

In their ultimate implications these two approaches are incompatible, and nothing reveals

O DEATH, WHERE IS THY STING?

better the confusion of Christians on this issue than the fact that today Christians accept both of them as equally valid and true. The problem of a secular hospital is solved by establishing a Christian chaplaincy in it, and the problem of a Christian hospital by making it as modern and scientific—that is, as "secular"— as possible. In fact, however, there is a progressive surrender of the religious approach to the secular, for reasons which we have already analyzed above. The modern minister tends to become not only an "assistant" to the medical doctor, but a "therapist" in his own right. All kinds of techniques of pastoral therapy, hospital visiting, care of the sick—which fill the catalogues of theological seminaries—are a good indication of this. But is this the *Christian approach*—and if it is not, are we simply to return to the old—the "religious" one?

The answer is no, it is not; but we are not simply to "return." We must discover the unchanging,

Trampling Down Death by Death

yet always contemporary, *sacramental* vision of man's life, and therefore of his suffering and disease—the vision that has been the Church's, even if we Christians have forgotten or misunderstood it.

The Church considers *healing* as a sacrament. But such was its misunderstanding during the long centuries of the total identification of the Church with "religion" (a misunderstanding from which all sacraments suffered, and the whole doctrine of sacraments) that the *sacrament of oil* became in fact the sacrament of death, one of the "last rites," opening to man a more or less safe passage into eternity. There is a danger that today, with the growing interest in healing among Christians, it will be understood as a sacrament of health, a useful "complement" to secular medicine. And both views are wrong, because both miss precisely the sacramental nature of this act.

O DEATH, WHERE IS THY STING?

A sacrament—as we already know—is always a *passage*, a *transformation*. Yet it is not a "passage" into "supernature," but into the kingdom of God, the world to come, into the very reality of this world and its life as redeemed and restored by Christ. It is the transformation not of "nature" into "supernature," but of the *old* into the *new*. A sacrament therefore is not a "miracle" by which God breaks, so to speak, the "laws of nature," but the manifestation of the ultimate Truth about the world and life, man and nature, the Truth which is Christ.

And healing is a sacrament because its purpose or end is not *health* as such, the restoration of physical health, but the *entrance* of man into the life of the kingdom, into the "joy and peace" of the Holy Spirit. In Christ everything in this world, and this means health and disease, joy and suffering, has become an ascension to, and entrance into this new life, its expectation and anticipation.

Trampling Down Death by Death

In this world suffering and disease are indeed "normal," but their very "normalcy" is abnormal. They reveal the ultimate and permanent defeat of man and of life, a defeat which no partial victories of medicine, however wonderful and truly miraculous, can ultimately overcome. But in Christ suffering is not "removed"; it is transformed into victory. The defeat *itself* becomes victory, a way, an entrance into the kingdom, and this is the only true *healing*.

Here is a man suffering on his bed of pain and the Church comes to him to perform the sacrament of healing. For this man, as for every man in the whole world, suffering can be defeat, the way of complete surrender to darkness, despair and solitude. It can be *dying* in the very real sense of the word. And yet it can be also the ultimate victory of Man and of Life in him. The Church does not come to restore *health* in this man, simply to replace medicine when medicine has exhausted its own possibilities. The Church

O DEATH, WHERE IS THY STING?

comes to take this man into the Love, the Light, and the Life of Christ. It comes not merely to "comfort" him in his sufferings, not to "help" him, but to make him a *martyr*, a *witness* to Christ in his very sufferings. A martyr is one who beholds "the heavens opened, and the Son of Man standing on the right hand of God" (Acts 7:56). A martyr is one for whom God is not another—and the last—chance to stop the awful pain; God is his very life, and thus everything in his life comes to God, and ascends to the fulness of Love.

In *this* world there shall be tribulation. Whether reduced to a minimum by man himself, or given some relief by the religious promise of a reward in the "other world," suffering remains here, it remains awfully "normal." And yet Christ says, "Be of good cheer, I have overcome the world" (Jn 16:33). Through his own suffering, not only has all suffering acquired a meaning but it has been given the power to become itself the sign,

Trampling Down Death by Death

the sacrament, the proclamation, the "coming" of that victory; the defeat of man, his very *dying* has become a way of Life.

* * *

The beginning of this victory is Christ's death. Such is the eternal gospel, and it remains "foolishness" not only for *this world*, but also for *religion* as long as it is the religion of this world ("lest the cross of Christ should be made of no effect"—1 Cor 1:17). The liturgy of Christian death does not begin when a man has come to the inescapable end and his corpse lies in church for the last rites while we stand around, the sad yet resigned witnesses of the dignified removal of a man from the world of the living. It begins every Sunday as the Church, ascending into heaven, "puts aside all earthly care"; it begins every feast day; it begins especially in the joy of Easter. The whole life of the Church is in a way the sacrament of our death, because all of it is

O DEATH, WHERE IS THY STING?

the proclamation of the Lord's death, the confession of his resurrection. And yet Christianity is not a death-centered religion; it is not a "mystery cult" in which an "objective" doctrine of salvation from death is offered to me in beautiful ceremonies and requires that I believe in it and thus profit from its "benefits."

To be Christian, to believe in Christ, means and has always meant this: to know in a transrational and yet absolutely certain way called faith, that Christ is the Life of all life, that he is Life itself and, therefore, *my* life. "In him was life; and the life was the light of men" (Jn 1:4) All Christian doctrines—those of the incarnation, redemption, atonement—are explanations, consequences, but not the "cause" of that faith. Only when we believe in Christ do all these affirmations become "valid" and "consistent." But faith itself is the acceptance not of this or that "proposition" about Christ, but of Christ himself as the Life and the light of life. For "the life was made

Trampling Down Death by Death

manifest, and we saw it, and testify to it, and proclaim to you the eternal life which was with the Father and was made manifest to us" (1 Jn 1:2). In this sense Christian faith is radically different from "religious belief." Its starting point is not "belief" but love. In itself and by itself all belief is partial, fragmentary, fragile. "For our knowledge is imperfect, and our prophecy is imperfect . . . as for prophecies, they will pass away; as for tongues, they will cease; as for knowledge, it will pass away." Only "*love never ends*" (1 Cor 13). And if to love someone means that I have my life in him, or rather that he has become the "content" of my life, to love Christ is to know and to possess him as the Life of my life.

Only this possession of Christ as Life, the "joy and peace" of communion with him, the certitude of his presence, makes meaningful the proclamation of Christ's death and the confession of his resurrection. In *this world* Christ's resurrection can never be made an "objective

O DEATH, WHERE IS THY STING?

fact." The risen Lord appeared to Mary and "she saw him standing and knew not it was Jesus." He stood on the shore of the Sea of Tiberias "but the disciples knew not it was Jesus." And on the way to Emmaus the eyes of the disciples "were kept from recognizing him." The preaching of the resurrection remains foolishness to this world, and no wonder even Christians themselves somehow "explain it away" by virtually reducing it to the old pre-Christian doctrines of immortality and survival. And indeed, if the doctrine of resurrection is just a "doctrine," if it is to be believed in as an event of the "future," as a mystery of the "other world," it is not substantially different from the other doctrines concerning the "other world" and can be easily confused with them. Whether it is the immortality of the soul or the resurrection of the body—I know nothing of them and all discussion here is mere "speculation." Death remains the same mysterious passage into a mysterious future. The *great joy* that the disciples felt when they saw the risen

Trampling Down Death by Death

Lord, that "burning of heart" that they experienced on the way to Emmaus were not because the mysteries of an "other world" were revealed to them, but because they saw the Lord. And he sent them to preach and to proclaim not the resurrection of the dead—not a doctrine of death—but repentance and remission of sins, the new life, the kingdom. They announced what they knew, that in Christ the *new life* has already begun, that he is Life Eternal, the Fulfilment, the Resurrection and the Joy of the world.

The Church is the entrance into the risen life of Christ; it is communion in life eternal, "joy and peace in the Holy Spirit." And it is the expectation of the "day without evening" of the kingdom; not of any "other world," but of the fulfilment of all things and all life in Christ. In him death itself has become an act of life, for he has filled it with himself, with his love and light. In him "all things are yours; whether . . . the world or life or death or the present or the future, all are yours; and you are Christ's; and Christ is God's" (1 Cor 3:21-23). And if I make this *new life* mine, mine this hunger and thirst for the kingdom, mine this expectation of Christ, mine the certitude that Christ is Life, then my very death will be an act of communion with Life. For neither life nor death can separate us from the love of Christ. I do not know when and how the fulfilment will come. I do not know when all things will be consummated in Christ. I know nothing about the "whens" and "hows." But I know that in Christ this great Passage, the *Pascha* of the world has begun, that the light of the "world to come" comes to us in the joy and peace of the Holy Spirit, for *Christ is risen and Life reigns.*

Finally I know that it is this faith and this certitude that fill with a joyful meaning the words of St Paul which we read each time we celebrate the "passage" of a brother or sister, one falling asleep in Christ:

Trampling Down Death by Death

For the Lord himself will descend from heaven with a cry of command with the archangel's call, and with the sound of the trumpet of God. And the dead in Christ will rise first, then we who are alive, who are left, shall be caught up together with them in the clouds to meet the Lord in the air; and so we shall always be with the Lord.

(1 Thess 4:16-17)

ABOUT THE AUTHOR

Father Alexander Schmemann was a prolific writer, brilliant lecturer and dedicated pastor. Former dean and professor of liturgical theology at St Vladimir's Orthodox Seminary, he passed away in 1983 at the age of sixty-two. Father Alexander Schmemann's insight into contemporary culture, church life, and liturgical celebration left an indelible mark on the Chrisitan community worldwide.

OTHER BOOKS BY
ALEXANDER SCHMEMANN
AVAILABLE FROM ST VLADIMIR'S SEMINARY PRESS

For the Life of the World

The Eucharist

Great Lent

Of Water and the Spirit

Liturgy and Tradition

Church, World, Mission

Celebration of Faith, vols 1, 2 & 3

Introduction to Liturgical Theology

The Historical Road of Eastern Orthodoxy

Ultimate Questions: An Anthology of Modern Russian Religious Thought

The Journals of Father Alexander Schmemann

Our Father